DECREES OF AETHELBERT

St. Aethelbert,

King of Kent

Translated by: D.P. Curtin

Dalcassian
Publishing
Company

PHILADELPHIA, PA

ISBN: **978-1-960069-78-8** (Paperback)

Library of Congress Control Number:
Author: Curtin, D.P. (1985-)

Printed by Ingram Content Group, 1 Ingram Blvd, La Vergne, Tennessee

First printing edition 2019.

Introduction

What follows is one of the oldest bodies of English law to survive. While there was clearly a body of edicts issued by prior Anglo-Saxon kings, they do not appear to have survived. It is exactly Aethelbert's special status as the first Christian English king that grants salience to this work. The edicts themselves are nothing unusual or extraordinary, yet they represent an early attempt at the codification of law, perhaps mimicking such efforts taking place in Constantinople at the time. While these laws only extend to a fraction of the English countryside, their very existence would set forth a precedent of the composition of English law. Moreover, this work would help cement the three-part marriage of monarch, law and church, which remains to this day.

D.P. Curtin
January 2, 2019
Wexford, PA

These are the judgments which King Aethelbert established in the days of Augustine.

I. The savings of God and of the Church shall be redeemed twelvefold. The bishop's treasure will be redeemed nine times. The savings of the priest shall be redeemed nine times. The deacon's savings shall be redeemed six times. The savings of the clergy shall be redeemed three times, the peace of the church shall be redeemed twice. The peace of the monastery will be redeemed twice.

II. If the king has called his people to him, and someone there has harmed them, he shall be compensated in two ways, and they shall pay the king 50 solidi.

III. If the king stays in someone's house, and someone does something wrong there, he shall make amends with double compensation.

IV. If a freedman takes something from the king by theft, he shall make up for it with a ninth compensation.

V. If someone kills a man in the king's town, he shall pay 50 solidi.

VI. If any man slay a freedman, the king shall receive 50 shillings for his possession.

VII. If any one kills the king's officers, the carpenters, or the butler's servants, he shall pay a moderate ordinary fine (leodgelde).

VIII. The king's patronage violated shall be compensated with 50 solidi.

IX. If a freedman steals anything from another freedman, he shall make amends threefold, and the king shall fine him of all his goods.

X. If any man lie with the virgin maidservant of the king, he shall redeem him with 50 solids.

XI. If the miller should keep them, he will buy them for 25 solidi, if they belong to the third lot, for 12 solidi.

XII. The king's cook will be compensated with 20 solidi.

XIII If any one of the count's town slays anyone, he shall compensate him with 12 solidi.

XIV. If any one has slept with the countess Pocillatrice, he shall pay 12 solidi.

XV. Any who violates the patronage of the plebeians will be paid 6 solidi.

XVI. If a man has intercourse with a plebeian concubine, he shall pay 6 solidi, for another slave he shall pay 50 scaettas, and for a third lot 30 scaettas.

XVII. If any one enters the house of another first, he shall buy 6 solidi. He who will enter second, 3 solidi, then each one a solidi.

XVIII. If any one adjusts arms to somewhere there is a quarrel, and no harm is done, he shall compensate with 6 solidi.

XIX. If a robbery has been committed, he will pay 6 solidi.

XX. And if any man kills another man, he shall pay 20 solidi.

XXI. If a man kills anyone, he shall pay the ordinary moderate fine of 100 shillings.

XXII. If a man kills someone at an open grave, he shall pay 20 shillings, and within 40 days he shall pay the whole ordinary fine.

XXIII. If the murderer goes out of the country, his relatives shall pay half the ordinary fine.

XXIV. If anyone wins the honest man, he shall compensate him with 20 shillings.

XXV. If any one of the plebeians kills a convict, he shall pay 6 solidi.

XXVI. If the guest kills the first convict, he will pay 80 solidi.

XXVII. And if he kills the second, he shall compensate him with 60 solidi, and the third with 40 solidi.

XXVIII. If a free man commits a violation of the fence, he shall pay 6 solidi.

XXIX. If any one takes away the thing kept within, he shall redeem it with threefold compensation.

XXX. If a freedman overcomes the septum, he will buy 4 solids.

XXXI. If any one kills anyone, he shall compensate each one in his own sense (*agene scaete*) and in good money.

XXXII. If a freedman has intercourse with the wife of a freedman, he shall redeem her with her capital, and he shall pay another wife with his own money, and he shall bring her to the other.

XXXIII. If a man pierces his right thigh with a spear, he shall make up for it with his value.

XXXIV. If the hair is caught, 50 cents is paid for the correction.

XXXV. If a bone appears, it will compensate for 3 solidi.

XXXVI. If the bone is injured, it will compensate for 4 solidi.

XXXVII. If it is completely broken, he will compensate with 10 solidi.

XXXVIII. If both are done, it will compensate for 20 solids.

XXXIX. If the shoulder is returned with a limp, he will make up 20 solidi.

XL. If the other ear hears nothing, he shall compensate with 25 solids.

XLI. If the ear is cut off, it will be bought for 12 solidi.

XLII. If the ear is pierced, it will compensate for 3 solidi.

XLIII. If the ear is clipped, it will be sold for 6 solidi.

XLIV. If the eye is shaken, it will compensate for 5 solidi.

XLV. If the mouth or the eye is affected by damage, it will be paid 20 solidi.

XLVI. If the nose is pierced, it will be paid for with 9 solidi.

XLVII. If there is one membrane, it will compensate for 3 solidi.

XLVIII. If both are pierced, it will be bought at 6 solidi.

XLIX. If each nose is clipped, each one will be sold for 6 solidi.

L. If they are pierced, it will be bought at 6 solidi.

LI. He that cut off the mouth of the mind, shall compensate with 20 solidi.

LII. For the four previous teeth, for each 6 solidi. For the tooth which is then next, 4 solids. For him who then stands next to him, 3 solidi, and thereafter for each one solidi;. If the speech becomes worse, 12 solidi. If the jaw is broken, 6 solids shall be compensated.

LIII. He who pierces the arm shall compensate with 6 solids. If the arm is broken, it will be bought for 6 solids.

LIV. If the thumb is cut off, 20 solidi. If the nails of the thumb are cut off, it shall be bought for 3 solidi. If one cuts off the index finger, he shall compensate with 8 solids. If someone cuts off the middle finger, he shall compensate with 4 solids. If anyone cuts off the ring finger, he shall compensate with 6 solids. And if any one cut off the smallest finger, he shall compensate with 11 solids.

LV. For each nail a solid will be compensated.

LVI. For the smallest ship 3 solidi, and for the larger 6 solidi.

LVII. If a man strikes the nose of another with his fist, 3 solidi.

LVIII. If it be a stroke, solid; if he receives a blow with an outstretched hand, he shall compensate with a solidi.

LIX. If the black mark is outside the clothes, he shall make amends with 30 skeits. If it is within the garments, each shall be bought for 20 shekels.

LX. If the diaphragm is wounded, he shall compensate with 12 solids. If it is pierced, he will pay 20 solids.

LXI. If a man is returned limping, he shall be redeemed for 30 solids.

LXII. If any one injures a callus, he shall make amends with 3 solids.

LXIII. If one's genital member is cut off, it shall be compensated by three times the ordinary fine. If it is broken, he will buy it for 6 solidi. If anyone falls, he shall compensate with 6 solidi.

LXIV. If the thigh is broken, it shall be compensated with 12 solidi. If he becomes lame, his friends must judge there.

LXV. If a rib is broken, he shall compensate with 3 solids.

LXVI. If anyone pierces the thigh, each incision shall be compensated with 6 solids. If it penetrates above the thumb, one solidi. For two inches two, above, three 3 solids are paid.
LXVII. If a vertebra is injured, it will be repaired with 3 solidi.
LXVIII. If a foot is amputated, it will be compensated by 50 solidi.

LXIX. If the big toe is amputated, it will be compensated with 10 solidi.

LXX. For the other toes of the foot, half the price shall be paid each, as was said of the fingers of the hand.

LXXI. If the toenails of the big toe are amputated, 30 scats will be used for correction, and 10 scats will be compensated for each of the others.

LXXII. If a free haired woman has done something dishonest, she will pay 30 solids.

LXXIII. The virgin's compensation should be as a man's child.

LXXIV. The violation of the patronage of the superior widow of a noble family will be redeemed with 50 solidi. Secondary 20 solids. The third 12 solidi. A quarter of 6 solidi.

LXXV. If a man marries a widow not of his own right, he shall make double compensation for the violation of the patronage.

LXXVI. If a man pays a price for a virgin, let her be bought, if it was done without deceit; but if there is a trick, he should be brought back home afterward, and his savings should be returned to him.

LXXVII. If she gives birth to a living child, she shall have half of the goods, if the husband dies first.

LXXVIII. If he wants to retire with his children, he has half the resources.

LXXIX. If the husband wants to have children, let them be like one of the children.

LXXX. If she has not borne a child, her relatives should have the property, she should have food, and a dowry.

LXXXI. If a man takes a virgin by force, he shall give the owner 50 shillings, and afterwards redeem her according to the will of the owner.

LXXXII. If she be betrothed to another in meti, she shall compensate him with 20 solidi.

LXXXIII. If she becomes pregnant, she pays 35 shillings, and 15 shillings to the king.

LXXXIV. If any man lies with the wife of a servant, while her husband is still alive, he shall make amends twice.

LXXXV. If a slave kills another innocent, he shall compensate with all means.

LXXXVI. If a servant's eye and foot are struck out, he shall be compensated for all his worth.

LXXXVII. If a man conquers the servant of another, he shall redeem him with 6 solidi.

LXXXVIII. The robbery of slaves is 3 solidi.

LXXXIX. If the servant be angry, he shall compensate with a double correction.

LATIN TEXT

Haec sunt judicia quae Ethelbertus rex constituit Augustini diebus.

I. Dei peculium et Ecclesiae duodecies emendetur; episcopi peculium undecies emendetur; sacerdotis peculium novies emendetur; diaconi peculium sexies emendetur; clerici peculium ter emendetur, ecclesiae pax bis emendetur; monasterii pax bis emendetur.

II. Si rex populum suum ad se vocaverit, et ipsis quis ibi malefecerit, dupliciter compensetur, et regi L solidi solvantur.

III. Si rex in alicujus domo convivetur, et ibi aliquis damni quid fecerit, duplici emendatione emendet.

IV. Si liber homo regi furto quid auferat, novena compensatione compenset.

V. Si in regis villa aliquis hominem occiderit, L solidis emendet.

VI. Si quis hominem liberum occiderit, rex L solidos pro dominio recipiat.

VII. Si quis regii praefecti fabrorum aut pincernae famulos occiderit, moderatam inulctam ordinariam (leodgelde) solvat.

VIII. Regis patrocinium violatum L solidis compensetur.

IX. Si liber homo a libero quid furetur, tripliciter emendet, et rex habeat mulctam, et omnia ejus bona.

X. Si quis cum regis ancilla virgine concubuerit, L solidis emendet.

XI. Si ea molens serva sit, XXV solidis emendet, si ea tertiae sortis, XII solidis.

XII. Regis obsonatrix XX solidis compensetur.

XIII. Si quis in comitis villa aliquem occiderit, XII solidis compenset.

XIV. Si cum comitis pocillatrice quis concubuerit, XII solidis compenset.

XV. Plebeii patrocinium violatum VI solidis emendetur.

XVI. Si cum plebeii pocillatrice quis concubuerit, VI solidis emendet, pro alia serva L scaettas, pro tertiae sortis XXX scaettas solvat.

XVII. Si quis in domum alicujus primus ingredietur, VI solidis emendet; qui secundus ingredietur, III solidis, deinde unusquisque solido.

XVIII. Si quis aliquibus arma accommodet ubi rixa est, et nihil mali patretur, VI solidis compenset.

XIX. Si latrocinium factum sit, VI solidis emendet.

XX. Si quis autem aliquem occiderit, XX solidis emendet.

XXI. Si quis aliquem occiderit, moderatam mulctam ordinariam C solidos compenset.

XXII. Si quis aliquem occiderit ad apertum sepulcrum, XX solidos compenset, et intra XL dies totam mulctam ordinariam compenset.

XXIII. Si homicida patria exierit, cognati ejus mediam ordinariam mulctam solvant.

XXIV. Si quis ingenuum hominem vinxerit, XX solidos compenset.

XXV. Si quis plebeii convictorem occiderit, VI solidis emendet.

XXVI. Si hospes autem occiderit primarium convictorem, LXXX solidis emendet.

XXVII. Si autem secundum occiderit, LX solidis compenset, tertium autem XL solidis compenset.

XXVIII. Si liber homo septi violationem fecerit, VI solidis emendet.

XXIX. Si quis rem intus servatam abstulerit, is triplici compensatione emendet.

XXX. Si liber homo septum superaverit, IV solidis emendet.

XXXI. Si quis aliquem occiderit, proprio sensu (agene scaete) et proba pecunia quemlibet compenset. XXXII. Si liber homo cum liberi hominis uxore concubuerit, ejus capitale redimat, et aliam uxorem propria pecunia mercetur, et illi alteri eam adducat.

XXXIII. Si quis dextrum femur lancea transpunxerit, valore suo illud compenset.

XXXIV. Si comae prehensio fiat, L scaettae ad emendationem solvantur.

XXXV. Si os appareat, III solidis compenset.

XXXVI. Si os laedatur, IV solidis compenset.

XXXVII. Si id penitus ipsi rumpatur, X solidis compenset.

XXXVIII. Si utrumque fiat, XX solidis compenset.

XXXIX. Si humerus claudicans reddatur, XX solidis compenset.

XL. Si altera auris nihil audit, XXV solidis compenset.

XLI. Si auris abscindatur, XII solidis emendetur.

XLII. Si auris perforetur, III solidis compenset.

XLIII. Si auris attondeatur, VI solidis emendetur.

XLIV. Si oculus excutiatur, L solidis compenset.

XLV. Si os aut oculus damno afficiatur, XX solidis emendetur.

XLVI. Si nasus perforetur, IX solidis emendetur.

XLVII. Si sit una membrana, III solidis compenset.

XLVIII. Si ambae perforatae sint, VI solidis emendetur.

XLIX. Si nares singulae attondeantur, unaquaeque VI solidis emendetur.

L. Si perforentur, VI solidis emendetur.

LI. Qui menti os absciderit, XX solidis compenset.

LII. Pro quatuor dentibus prioribus, pro singulis VI solidi; pro dente qui tunc proximus est, IV solidi; pro eo qui tunc juxta stat, III solidi, et deinceps pro singulis solidus; si elocutio deterior fiat, XII solidi; si maxilla fracta fuerit, VI solidi compensentur.

LIII. Qui brachium pertundit, VI solidis compenset. Si brachium fractum fuerit, VI solidis emendetur.

LIV. Si pollex abscindatur, XX solidis; si pollicis unguis abscindatur, III solidis emendetur; si quis indicem digitum absciderit, VIII solidis compenset; si quis medium digitum absciderit, IV solidis compenset; si quis digitum annularem absciderit, VI solidis compenset; si quis autem minimum digitum absciderit, XI solidis compenset.

LV. Pro unguibus singulis solidus compensetur.

LVI. Pro minimo naevo III solidi, et pro majoribus VI solidi.

LVII. Si quis alteri pugno nasum verberet, III solidi. LVIII. Si plaga sit, solido; si elata manu plagam exceperit, solido compenset.

LIX. Si plaga nigra sit extra vestes, XXX scaettis emendet; si sit intra vestes, quaelibet XX scaettis emendetur.

LX. Si diaphragma vulneretur, XII solidis compenset; si perforetur, XX solidis emendet.

LXI. Si quis claudicans reddatur, XXX solidis emendetur.

LXII. Si callum quis vulneraverit, III solidis emendet.

LXIII. Si cui genitale membrum abscindatur, triplici mulcta ordinaria illud compensetur; si pertusum sit, VI solidis emendet; si quis inciderit, VI solidis compenset.

LXIV. Si femur ruptum fuerit, XII solidis compensetur; si is claudus fiat, ibi amici judicare debent.

LXV. Si costa rumpatur, III solidis compenset.

LXVI. Si femur quis transpunxerit, quaelibet incisio VI solidis compensetur; si supra pollicem penetret, solido; pro duobus pollicibus duo, supra, tres III solidi solvantur.

LXVII. Si vertebra vulneretur, III solidis emendetur.

LXVIII. Si pes amputetur, L solidis compensetur.

LXIX. Si major digitus pedis amputetur, X solidis compensetur. LXX. Pro aliis digitis pedis singulis dimidium pretii, sicuti de digitis manus dictum est, solvatur.

LXXI. Si majoris digiti pedis unguis amputetur, XXX scaettae ad emendationem, pro caeteris singulis X scaettae compensentur.

LXXII. Si libera femina capillata inhonesti quid fecerit, XXX solidis emendet. LXXIII. Virginis compensatio sit ut liberi hominis.

LXXIV. Patrocinium violatum potioris viduae nobilis familiae L solidis emendetur; secundariae XX solidis; tertiae XII solidis; quartae VI solidis.

LXXV. Si quis viduam non sui juris duxerit, bis compenset patrocinium violatum.

LXXVI. Si vir virginem mercetur pretio, empta sit, si sine dolo factum sit; si autem dolus subest, postea domum reducatur, et illi peculium suum reddatur.

LXXVII. Si ipsa vivum fetum pepererit, medietatem bonorum habeat, si vir ante moriatur.

LXXVIII. Si cum liberis recedere velit, dimidium facultatum habeat.

LXXIX. Si maritus habere velit liberos, sint ipsi sicuti unus liberorum.

LXXX. Si ipsa prolem non pepererit, cognati bona habeant, ipsa alimenta, et dotem.

LXXXI. Si quis virginem per vim ceperit, possessori L solidos det, et postea secundum possessoris voluntatem eam redimat.

LXXXII. Si ea alteri in pretio desponsata sit, XX solidis compenset.

LXXXIII. Si gravida fuerit, XXXV solidos, et regi XV solidos solvat.

LXXXIV. Si quis cum servi uxore concubuerit, vivo marito, bis emendet.

LXXXV. Si servus alterum occiderit innocentem, omnibus facultatibus compenset.

LXXXVI. Si servi oculus et pes excutiatur, omni valore compensetur.

LXXXVII. Si quis servum alicujus vinxerit, VI solidis emendet.

LXXXVIII. Servi latrocinium sit III solidi.

LXXXIX. Si servus furetur, duplici emendatione compenset.

THE
SCRIPTORIUM
PROJECT

D A L C A S S I A N
PUBLISHING COMPANY
Philadelphia, PA

The Scriptorium Project is the work of a small group of lay people of various apostolic churches who are interested in the preservation, transmission, and translation of the works of the early and medieval church. Our efforts are to make the works of the church fathers accessible to anyone who might have an interest in Christian antiquities and the theological, philosophical, and moral writings that have become the bedrock of Western Civilization.

To-date, our releases have pulled from the Greek, Syriac, Georgian, Latin, Celtic, Ethiopian, and Coptic traditions of Christianity, and have been pulled from sundry local traditions and languages.

Other Titles and Translations by D.P. Curtin:

First Book of Ethiopian Maccabees (2018)
Chronicon by Eutrandus of Ticino (2019)
Decrees of Aethelbert by St. Aethelbert, King of Kent (2019)
The Measure to be taxed for Penance by St. Columba of Iona (2019)
Protoevangelium of James: Greek and English Texts (2019)
Edicts of the Synod of Paris by Chlothar II, King of Franks (2019)
The Life of St. Desiderius by Sisebut, King of Visigoths (2019)
The Synod of Rome by St. Boniface IV of Rome (2019)
Letter to Pope Theodore by Victor of Carthage (2020)
The Decree of 610 by Gundemar, King of Visigoths (2020)
Laws of the Church by Chlothar III, King of Franks (2020)
Donations by St. Aethelbert, King of Kent (2020)
The Mystical Interpretation by St. Aileran the Wise (2020)
Laws of the Church by St. Dagobert II, King of Franks (2020)
The Old Nubian Miracle of St. Mena (2021)
About Fifteen Problems by St. Albertus Magnus (2022)
Testament of Some Former Things by John Scotus Eriugena (2022)
The Georgian Synaxarium (2022)
Instructions: Counsel for Novices by St. Ammonas the Hermit (2022)
The Syriac Menologium and Martyrology (2022)
Book on Religious Exercise and Quiet by St. Isaiah the Solitary (2022)
Vision of Theophilus by St. Cyril of Alexandria (2022)
On Fate (De Fato) by St. Albertus Magnus (2023)
Fragments of 'Chronicle' by Hippolytus of Thebes (2023)
Life of the Blessed Theotokos by Epiphanius Monachus (2023)
Syriac Life of John the Baptist by Serapion the Presbyter (2023)
Second Book of Ethiopian Maccabees (2023)